AAT

Principles of Bookkeeping Controls

Pocket Notes

These Pocket Notes support study for the following AAT qualifications:

AAT Level 2 Certificate in Accounting

AAT Level 2 Certificate in Bookkeeping

AAT Certificate in Accounting at SCQF Level 6

KAPLAN

PUBLISHING

British library cataloguing-in-publication data

A catalogue record for this book is available from the British Library.

Published by:
Kaplan Publishing UK
Unit 2 The Business Centre
Molly Millars Lane
Wokingham
Berkshire
RG41 2QZ

ISBN 978-1-83996-597-5

© Kaplan Financial Limited, 2023

Printed and bound in Great Britain.

CONTENTS

Preface

These Pocket Notes contain the key things that you need to know for the exam, presented in a unique visual way that makes revision easy and effective.

Written by experienced lecturers and authors, these Pocket Notes break down content into manageable chunks to maximise your concentration.

Quality and accuracy are of the utmost importance to us so if you spot an error in any of our products, please send an email to mykaplanreporting@kaplan.com with full details, or follow the link to the feedback form in MyKaplan.

Our Quality Co-ordinator will work with our technical team to verify the error and take action to ensure it is corrected in future editions.

A guide to the assessment

The assessment

Principles of Bookkeeping Controls (POBC) is the second of two financial accounting assessments at Level 2 Certificate in Accounting, building on the knowledge and skills from Introduction to Bookkeeping (ITBK).

ITBK should be completed prior to commencement of your POBC studies.

Examination

POBC is assessed by means of a Computer-Based Assessment (CBA) comprised of 8 tasks. The time allowed for the CBA is 1½ hours.

In any one assessment, learners may not be assessed on all content, or on the full depth or breadth of a piece of content. The content assessed may change over time to ensure validity of assessment, but all assessment criteria will be tested over time.

Learning outcomes & weighting

1.	Use control accounts	25%
2.	Reconcile a bank statement with the cash book	25%
3.	Use the journal	25%
4.	Produce trial balances	25%
	Total	100%

Pass mark

To pass a unit assessment, students need to achieve a mark of 70% or more.

This unit contributes 25% of the total amount required for the Foundation Certificate in Accounting qualification.

Double entry bookkeeping

- Principles of double entry bookkeeping.
- Accounting equation.
- Ledger accounts.
- General rules of double entry bookkeeping.
- Accounting for cash transactions.
- Accounting for credit transactions.
- Balancing ledger accounts.
- Preparing a trial balance.

Principles of double entry bookkeeping

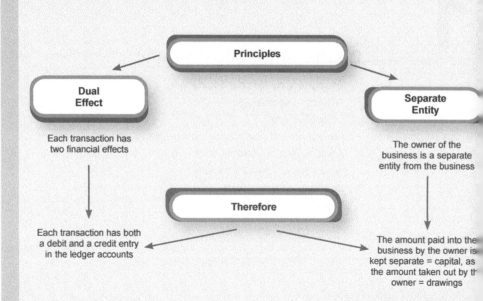

Accounting equation

Assets – Liabilities = Capital

Terminology

Asset Something owned by the business	**Liability** Something owed by the business	**Capital** Amount the owner has invested in the business	**Receivable** Someone who owes the business money	**Payable** Someone the business owes money to

Ledger accounts

Typical ledger account:

Title of account

Date	Narrative	£	Date	Narrative	£
	Debit side	x		**Credit** side	x

The dual effect means that every transaction is recorded as a debit in one account and a credit in another account.

Key question – which account is the debit entry to and which account is the credit entry to?

General rules of double entry bookkeeping

Ledger account

Debit	Credit
Money in	Money out
Increase in asset	Increase in liability
Decrease in liability	Decrease in asset
Increase in expense	Increase in income

Accounting for cash transactions

Examples of ledger accounting:

(i) Payment of £10,000 into business bank account by owner:

Debit Cash (money in)

Credit Capital (increase in liability – amount owed to owner)

Cash account

	£		£
Capital	10,000		

Capital account

	£		£
		Cash	10,000

(ii) Purchase of goods for cash of £3,000:

Debit Purchases (expense)

Credit Cash (money out)

Purchases account

	£		£
Cash	3,000		

Cash account

	£		£
		Purchases	3,000

Accounting for credit transactions

(i) Purchases goods for £6,000 on credit

   Debit Purchases (expense)

   Credit Trade Payables (liability)

Purchase account

	£		£
Trade payables	6,000		

Trade payables account

	£		£
		Purchases	6,000

(ii) Sale of goods on credit for £8,000

   Debit Trade Receivables (asset)

   Credit Sales Revenue (income)

Trade receivables account

	£		
Sales	8,000		

Sales account

	£		
		Receivables	8,00

(iii) Payment of part of money owed to credit supplier of £1,500

Debit Trade payables (reduction in liability)

Credit Cash (money out)

Trade payables account

	£		£
Cash	1,500		

Cash account

	£		£
		Trade payables	1,500

(iv) Receipt of part of money owed by credit customer of £5,000

Debit Cash (money in)

Credit Trade receivables (reduction in asset)

Cash account

	£		£
Trade receivables	5,000		

Trade receivables account

	£		£
		Cash	5,000

Balancing ledger accounts

At various points in time the owner/owners of a business will need information about the total transactions in the period. Eg, total sales, amount of payables outstanding, amount of cash remaining. This can be found by balancing the ledger accounts.

Here is a typical cash (or bank) account:

Cash account

	£		£
Capital	10,000	Purchases	3,000
Sales	4,000	Rent	500
Receivables	5,000	Payables	1,500

Step 1 Total both debit and credit side and make a note of the totals.

Step 2 Insert higher of totals as total for both sides (leaving a line before inserting totals).

Cash account

	£		£
Capital	10,000	Purchases	3,00
Sales	4,000	Rent	50
Receivables	5,000	Payables	1,50
	19,000		19,00

Step 3 On side with smaller total insert figur which makes it add up to total and call this the balance carried down (balance c/d).

Cash account

	£		£
Capital	10,000	Purchases	3,00
Sales	4,000	Rent	50
Receivables	5,000	Payables	1,50
		Balance c/d	14,00
	19,000		19,00

Step 4 On the opposite side of the account enter this same figure below the total line and call it the balance brought down (balance b/d).

In the assessment you will be required to balance a number of ledger accounts.

Cash account

	£		£
Capital	10,000	Purchases	3,000
Sales	4,000	Rent	500
Receivables	5,000	Payables	1,500
		Balance c/d	14,000
	19,000		19,000
Balance b/d	14,000		

This shows that after all of these transactions there is £14,000 of cash left as an asset in the business (a debit balance = an asset).

Preparing a trial balance

What is a trial balance?

- list of all of the ledger balances in the general ledger
- debit balances and credit balances are listed separately
- debit balance total should equal credit balance total.

Example		

Simple trial balance

	Debit £	Credit £
Sales		5,000
Wages	100	
Purchases	3,000	
Rent	200	
Vehicle	3,000	
Receivables	100	
Payables		1,400
	6,400	6,400

Debit or credit balance?

If you are just given a list of balances you must know whether they are debit or credit balances.

Remember the rules!

Debit Balances	Credit Balances
Assets	Liabilities
Expenses	Income

12

Sales and purchases returns

Sales returns = debit balance
(opposite to sales)

Purchases returns = credit balance (opposite
to purchases)

Discounts allowed and discounts received

Discounts allowed = debit balance (expense)

Discounts received = credit balance (opposite
of an expense)

CBA focus

Returns and discounts are not as obvious as
other accounts as to whether they are debit
or credit balances so make sure that you
understand the logic behind these balances.

2

Control account reconciliations

- Sales ledger control account.
- Sales ledger control account reconciliation.
- Purchases ledger control account.
- Purchases ledger control account reconciliation.
- VAT control accounts.

Sales ledger control account

- total receivables account
- sales invoices posted from sales day book
- credit notes posted from sales returns day book
- receipts from customers posted from cash receipts book.

Example

Writing up the sales ledger control account

The opening balance at 1 May on the sales ledger control account is £3,400.

Sales ledger control account

	£		£
Opening balance	3,400		

Asset – debit balance

- total from sales day book for month of May £20,600

Sales ledger control account

	£		£
Opening balance	3,400		
SDB	20,600		

Full double entry:

Debit   Sales ledger control account

Credit   Sales and VAT accounts

- total from sales returns day book for month of May £1,800

Sales ledger control account

	£		£
Opening balance	3,400	SRDB	1,800
SDB	20,600		

Full double entry:

Debit Sales returns and VAT accounts

Credit Sales ledger control account

- total from receivables column in cash receipts book of £19,500

Sales ledger control account

	£		£
Opening balance	3,400	SRDB	1,800
SDB	20,600	CRB	19,500

Full double entry:

Debit Cash book

Credit Sales ledger control account

- total of discounts allowed column in Discounts Allowed Daybook (DADB) £1,200.

Sales ledger control account

	£		£
Opening balance	3,400	SRDB	1,800
SDB	20,600	CRB	19,500
		DADB	1,200

Full double entry:

Debit   Discounts allowed account

Credit Sales ledger control account

Other entries to the sales ledger control account

There are two other potential entries in the sales ledger control account:

- irrecoverable debts written off – when a debt is highly unlikely to be received
- contra entry – when money is owed to a supplier who is also a customer and therefore owes money – the two amounts are set off against each other.

Note that both of these entries are credits to the Sales Ledger Control Account, reducing the balance due.

Example

Irrecoverable debts written off

- a customer owing £400 has gone into liquidation and therefore it has been decided to write this debt off as bad.

Sales ledger control account

	£		£
Opening balance	3,400	SRDB	1,800
SDB	20,600	CRB	19,500
		DADB	1,200
		Irrecoverable debt expense	400

Full double entry:

Debit   Irrecoverable debt expense account

Credit   Sales ledger control account

Example continued – contra entry

- a customer who owes us £200 is also a supplier and we owe him £300. It has been agreed that the two amounts should be set off by a contra entry leaving only £100 owed by us to the supplier.

Sales ledger control account

	£		£
Opening balance	3,400	SRDB	1,800
SDB	20,600	CRB	19,500
		DADB	1,200
		Irrecoverable debt write off	400
		Contra	200

Full double entry:

Debit   Purchases ledger control account

Credit   Sales ledger control account

Example continued – balancing the sales ledger control account

Sales ledger control account

	£		£
Opening balance	3,400	SRDB	1,800
SDB	20,600	CRB	19,500
		DADB	1,200
		Irrecoverable debt write off	400
		Contra	200
		Balance c/d	900
	24,000		24,000
Balance b/d	900		

This shows that at the end of May we have total receivables of £900.

Sales ledger control account reconciliation

- the sales ledger control account is written up using totals from the sales day book, sales returns day book and cash receipts book

- individual accounts for receivables in the subsidiary sales ledger are written up using the individual entries from the sales day book, sales returns day book and cash receipts book

- as both are written up from the same sources of information, at the end of the period the balance on the sales ledger control account should equal the total of the list of balances in the subsidiary sales ledger.

SLCA balance = Total of list of subsidiary sales ledger

Purpose of sales ledger control account reconciliation

- to show that SLCA does in fact equal the total of the list of balances

- to indicate that there are errors in either the SLCA or the subsidiary sales ledger accounts if the two are not equal

- to find the correct figure for total receivables to appear in the trial balance.

Preparing a sales ledger control account reconciliation

Step 1

- Extract list of balances from subsidiary sales ledger accounts and total.

Step 2

- Balance the sales ledger control account.

Step 3

- If the two figures are different the reasons for the difference must be investigated.

Step 4

- correct any errors that affect the sales ledger control account
- find corrected balance on sales ledger control account.

Step 5

- correct any errors that affect the total of the list of balances from the subsidiary sales ledger
- find corrected total of list of subsidiary sales ledger balances.

Example

Sales ledger control account reconciliation

The balance on the sales ledger control account at 31 May is £4,100. The individual balances on the subsidiary sales ledger are as follows:

	£
Receivable A	1,200
Receivable B	300
Receivable C	2,000
Receivable D	1,000

Step 1

- **Extract list of balances from subsidiary sales ledger accounts and total**

	£
Receivable A	1,200
Receivable B	300
Receivable C	2,000
Receivable D	1,000
	4,500

Step 2

- **Balance the sales ledger control account**

The balance has been given as £4,100.

Step 3

- **If the two figures are different the reasons for the difference must be investigated**

You are given the following information:

- a page of the sales day book had been undercast by £100

- a credit note for £50 to Receivable A had been entered into A's subsidiary sales ledger account as an invoice

- a contra entry with Receivable B for £200 had only been entered in the sales ledger control account and not the individual subsidiary sales ledger account.

Step 4

- correct any errors that affect the sales ledger control account
- find corrected balance on sales ledger control account.

Sales ledger control account

	£		£
Original balance	4,100		
SDB undercast	100	Correct balance	4,200
CPB	4,200		
			4,200
	4,200		4,200
Correct balance	4,200		

If the sales day book was undercast then the amount posted to the sales ledger control account was £100 too small and therefore an additional debit entry for £100 is needed in the control account.

The other two adjustments affect the individual accounts not the control account.

Step 5

- correct any errors that affect the total of the list of balances from the subsidiary sales ledger
- find corrected total of list of subsidiary sales ledger balances.

	£
Total list of balances	4,500
Less: Credit note entered as invoice	(100)
Less: Contra	(200)
Corrected list of balances	4,200

As the credit note for £50 had been entered as an invoice, the list of balances must be reduced by £100 to reflect the removal of the invoice and the entry of the credit note.

The contra had only been entered in the sales ledger control account therefore £200 must be deducted from the list of balances.

Credit balances on sales ledger accounts

- normally a receivable's balance on their subsidiary sales ledger account will be a debit balance brought down
- sometimes however the balance will be a credit balance.

Reasons for credit balance:

Overpayment by receivable

Misposting to subsidiary sales ledger account

Treatment of credit balance

- when the list of subsidiary sales ledger balances is drawn up and totalled, the credit balance must be deducted rather than added.

Purchases ledger control account

- total payables account
- purchase invoices posted from purchases day book
- credit notes posted from purchases returns day book
- payments to suppliers posted from cash payments book
- discounts received from discounts received day book.

Example

Writing up the purchases ledger control account

- the opening balance at 1 May on the purchases ledger control account is £2,100

Purchases ledger control account

	£		£
		Opening balance	2,100

Liability – credit balance

- total from purchases day book for month of May £15,800

Purchases ledger control account

	£		£
		Opening balance	2,100
		PDB	15,800

Full double entry:

Debit   Purchases and VAT accounts

Credit   Purchases ledger control account

- total from purchases returns day book for month of May £900

Purchases ledger control account

	£		£
PRDB	900	Opening balance	2,100
		PDB	15,800

Full double entry:

Debit   Purchases ledger control account

Credit   Purchases returns and VAT accounts

- total from payables column in cash payments book of £13,000

Purchases ledger control account

	£		£
PRDB	900	Opening balance	2,100
CPB	13,000	PDB	15,800

Full double entry:

Debit Purchases ledger control account

Credit Cash Book

- total of discounts received column in Discounts Received Daybook (DRDB) £700

Purchases ledger control account

	£		£
PRDB	900	Opening balance	2,100
CPB	13,000	PDB	15,800
DRDB	700		

Full double entry:

Debit Purchases ledger control account

Credit Discounts received account

- a customer who owes us £200 is also a supplier and we owe him £300. It has been agreed that the two amounts should be set off by a contra entry leaving only £100 owed by us to the supplier

Purchases ledger control account

	£		£
PRDB	900	Opening balance	2,100
CPB	13,000	PDB	15,800
DRDB	700		
Contra	200		

Full double entry:

Debit Purchases ledger control account

Credit Sales ledger control account

Balancing the purchases ledger control account

Purchases ledger control account

	£		£
PRDB	900	Opening balance	2,100
CPB	13,000	PDB	15,800
DRDB	700		
Contra	200		
Balance c/d	3,100		
	17,900		17,900
		Balance b/d	3,100

This shows that we have payables totalling £3,100 at the end of May.

CBA focus

In the examination you will have to know the accounting entries for both the sales ledger control account and the purchases ledger control account.

Purchases ledger control account reconciliation

- the purchases ledger control account is written up using totals from the purchases day book, purchases returns day book and cash payments book

- individual accounts for payables in the subsidiary purchases ledger are written up using the individual entries from the purchases day book, purchases returns day book and cash payments book

- as both are written up from the same sources of information then at the end of the period the balance on the purchases ledger control account should equal the total of the list of balances in the subsidiary purchases ledger.

> PLCA balance = Total of list of subsidiary purchases ledger

Purpose of purchases ledger control account reconciliation

- to show that the PLCA does in fact equal the total of the list of balances

- to indicate that there are errors in either the PLCA or the subsidiary purchases ledger accounts if the two are not equal

- to find the correct figure for total payables to appear in the trial balance.

Preparing a purchases ledger control account reconciliation

Step 1

- Extract list of balances from subsidiary purchases ledger accounts and total.

Step 2

- Balance the purchases ledger control account.

Step 3
- If the two figures are different the reasons for the difference must be investigated.

Step 4
- correct any errors that affect the purchases ledger control account
- find corrected balance on the purchases ledger control account.

Step 5
- correct any errors that affect the total of the list of balances from the subsidiary purchases ledger
- find corrected total of list of subsidiary purchases ledger balances.

Example

Purchases ledger control account reconciliation

The balance on the purchases ledger control account at 31 May is £2,000. The individual balances on the subsidiary purchases ledger are as follows:

	£
Payable E	800
Payable F	600
Payable G	400
Payable H	700

Step 1

- **Extract list of balances from subsidiary purchases ledger accounts and total**

	£
Payable E	800
Payable F	600
Payable G	400
Payable H	700
	2,500

Step 2

- **Balance the purchases ledger control account**

  The balance has been given as £2,000.

Step 3

- **If the two figures are different the reasons for the difference must be investigated.**

You are given the following information:

- a page of the purchases returns day book had been overcast by £1,000

- discounts received from suppliers totalling £680 had not been posted to the control account

- an invoice to payable G for £350 had been entered into the individual account in the subsidiary purchases ledger as £530.

Step 4

- correct any errors that affect the purchases ledger control account
- find corrected balance on purchases ledger control account.

Purchases ledger control account

	£		£
Discounts received	680	Original balance	2,000
Corrected balance	2,320	PRDB overcast	1,000
	3,000		3,000
		Corrected balance	2,320

If the purchases returns day book was overcast then the amount posted to the purchases ledger control account on the debit side for returns was £1,000 too big

and therefore an additional credit entry for £1,000 is needed in the control account.

The discounts received of £680 were omitted from the control account therefore the control account must be debited with this amount.

Step 5

- correct any errors that affect the total of the list of balances from the subsidiary purchases ledger
- find corrected total of list of subsidiary purchases ledger balances.

	£
Total list of balances	2,500
Less: transposition error on invoice (530 – 350)	(180)
Corrected total list of balances	2,320

The invoice had been entered as £180 higher than it should have been and therefore the total of the list of balances must reduced by £180.

Example

Sales ledger control account reconciliation

	£
Balance per sales ledger control account	4,580
Total of list of subsidiary sales ledger balances	4,780
Difference	200

In this case the list of balances is £200 higher than the control account total. What may have caused this?

Suppose that one balance in the list of balances is for £100. It is possible that this is in fact a credit balance of £100 but has been incorrectly added into the list of balances rather than being deducted.

Alternatively if the control account includes an irrecoverable debt write off of £200 then it is possible that this has not been entered into the individual account in the subsidiary sales ledger causing the subsidiary sales ledger balances to be higher than the control account balance.

In the examination you will always have to prepare a sales or purchases ledger control account reconciliation. The style of these questions is as follows:

(i) Write up the sales/purchases ledger control account.

(ii) Total the list of balances.

(iii) Compare the balance on the control account to the total list of balances and determine the difference.

(iv) Identify what the difference may have been caused by.

Look for numbers in the control account or list of balances which either equal the difference identified or is twice as much as the difference and this could be the cause of the difference.

VAT control accounts

As the sales, sales returns, purchases and purchases returns are entered into the accounts, the VAT is also calculated and accounted for.

You may be given extracts from the day books and asked to enter the relevant figures into the VAT control account, or you may be asked to list the entries required to the control account indicating whether they would be on the debit or credit side of the VAT control account.

It may also be a requirement to find the overall balance of the VAT control account i.e. to state what the balance is and whether it is owed to the tax authorities (HMRC) or whether a refund is due from them. The illustration above has shown us the VAT control account assuming that the balance brought down is on the credit side and therefore a liability. Although it is less likely, you may also encounter a VAT control account where the balance brought down is on the debit side and therefore an asset, meaning a refund is due to the business from the tax authorities.

VAT control account

	£		£
VAT on credit purchases		VAT on credit sales	
VAT on cash purchases		VAT on cash sales	
VAT on sales returns		VAT on purchases returns	
Balance c/d	_____		_____
	_____		_____
		Balance b/d	

3

Errors and suspense accounts

- What is a trial balance?
- Errors.
- Journal entries.
- Suspense account.
- Correcting errors and clearing the suspense account.

What is a trial balance?

- list of all of the ledger balances in the general ledger
- debit balances and credit balances listed in separate columns
- the total of the debit balances should equal the total of the credit balances.

Example

Trial balance

	Debit balances £	Credit balances £
Sales		5,000
Wages	100	
Purchases	3,000	
Rent	200	
Car	3,000	
Receivables	100	
Payables		1,400
	6,400	6,400

Debit or credit balance?

If you are just given a list of balances you must know whether they are debit or credit balances.

Remember the rules!

In the examination you will either have to enter a number of balances in the trial balance from ledger accounts that have been balanced or you will be given a list of balances that you then have to determine which side of the trial balance they should appear on.

Debit balances	Credit balances
Expense	Liability
Asset	Income
Drawings	Capital

Errors

In a manual accounting system errors will be made – some are identified by extracting a trial balance but others are not.

Single entry
only one side of an entry made

Casting error
account incorrectly balanced

Errors identified by extracting a trial balance

Transposition error
numbers transposed in recording e.g. 98 shown as 89

Extraction error
account balance entered on trial balance as wrong figure

Did you know? A transposition error can be identified by the difference being exactly divisible by 9!

Errors not identified by extracting a trial balance

Errors of original entry
error made when transaction first entered into primary records

Errors of omission
a transaction is not entered at all in the primary records

Compensation errors
two or more errors which are exactly equal and opposite

Errors of principle
entry made in fundamentally wrong type of account e.g. revenue expense entered into capital/non-current asset account

Errors of commission
entry made in wrong account although account of the correct type e.g. rent expense entered into electricity expense account

Journal entries

- written instruction to bookkeeper to put through a double entry which has not been sourced from the books of prime entry
- used for correction of errors/adjustments/ unusual items
- only used for adjusting double entry errors in the general ledger – not used for entries in the subsidiary sales or subsidiary purchases ledgers.

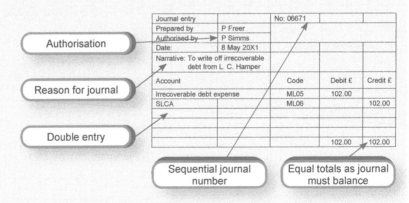

Journal entry		No: 06671		
Prepared by	P Freer			
Authorised by	P Simms			
Date:	8 May 20X1			
Narrative: To write off irrecoverable debt from L. C. Hamper				
Account		Code	Debit £	Credit £
Irrecoverable debt expense		ML05	102.00	
SLCA		ML06		102.00
			102.00	102.00

Authorisation

Reason for journal

Double entry

Sequential journal number

Equal totals as journal must balance

Suspense account

Used in two circumstances

Bookkeeper does not know one side of an entry therefore posts it to a suspense account

When trial balance totals disagree used to temporarily balance the trial balance

Example
£200 received but bookkeeper does not know what it is for so debits cash receipts book and credits suspense account

Example
Total of debit balances on trial balance is £35,000 but total of credit balances is £34,000. 1,000 credited to suspense account to make trial balance totals equal

Correcting errors and clearing the suspense account

- errors corrected by putting through a journal for the correcting entry.

How to find correcting entry

- work out the double entry that has been done
- work out the double entry that should have been done
- draft journal entry to go from what has been done to what should have been done.

CBA focus

In the examination have these 3 questions to mind..

(1) What has been done?

(2) What should have been done?

(3) How do we correct it?

Example

journal entries

(i) An amount of £200 for electricity bill payments was entered into the rent account.

What has been done?

Debit	Rent account	£200
Credit	Bank account	£200

What should have been done?

Debit	Electricity account	£200
Credit	Bank account	£200

How do we correct it? – Journal entry

Debit	Electricity account	£200
Credit	Rent account	£200

(ii) A purchase invoice for £1,000 had not been entered into the books of prime entry.

What has been done?

No entries at all

What should have been done?

Debit	Purchases account	£1,000
Credit	Purchases ledger control account	£1,000

How do we correct it? – Journal entry

Debit	Purchases account	£1,000
Credit	Purchases ledger control account	£1,000

(iii) An irrecoverable debt for £100 is to be written off.

This is not correction of an error but an adjustment to be made.

Journal entry

Debit	Irrecoverable debt expense account	£100
Credit	Sales ledger control account	£100

(iv) A contra entry for £500 has been entered in the general ledger control accounts but has not been entered in the subsidiary purchases ledger.

No journal entry is required as the error is not in the general ledger but the subsidiary ledger. However the payable's account in the subsidiary purchases ledger and the receivable's account in the subsidiary sales ledger must be adjusted to reflect this contra entry.

CBA focus

In most examinations you will be required to draft journal entries to correct errors.

Errors and the suspense account

Some errors made will affect the trial balance and therefore are part of the suspense account balance.

Example

(i) Discounts allowed of £150 have been entered as a credit entry in the discounts allowed account

What has been done?

Credit	Discounts allowed account	£150
Credit	Sales ledger control account	£150

What should have been done?

Debit	Discounts allowed account	£150
Credit	Sales ledger control account	£150

How do we correct it? – Journal entry

Debit	Discounts allowed account	£300
Credit	Suspense account	£300

The discounts allowed account has been credited rather than debited with £150 therefore to turn this into a debit of £150 it needs to be debited with £300. No other account is incorrect so the other side of the entry is to the suspense.

(ii) The balance for motor expenses of £400 has been omitted from the trial balance.

What has been done?

The motor expenses balance of £400 has been omitted from the trial balance.

What should be done?

A £400 debit balance (expense) must appear on the trial balance.

How do we correct it? – Journal entry

Debit   Motor expenses (TB)   £400

Credit   Suspense account   £400

Clearing the suspense account

The suspense account cannot remain as a permanent account and must be investigated and cleared before the accounts are prepared.

KAPLAN PUBLISHING

Example

A business has a suspense account with a debit balance of £80.

The following errors were noted:

(i) rent of £750 was entered into the rent account as £570

(ii) an advertising bill was overstated in the advertising account by £100

Journals

(i)	Debit	Rent account	£180
	Credit	Suspense account	£180
(ii)	Debit	Suspense account	£100
	Credit	Advertising account	£100

Suspense account			
	£		£
Opening balance	80		
Advertising	100	Rent	180
	180		180

The suspense account is now cleared.

CBA focus

In most examinations you will be required to draft journal entries to clear a suspense account balance but usually there are only two adjustments required to be made to clear the balance.

Payroll procedures

- Gross pay and deductions.
- Total wages cost.
- Paying wages and salaries.
- Accounting for wages and salaries.
- Paying PAYE and NIC.

Gross pay and deductions

Gross pay

Made up of:

Basic wage + overtime + bonus + shift payment + commission etc.

Net pay

	£
Gross pay	X
Less: PAYE	(X)
Less: Employee's NIC	(X)
Less: other deductions	(X)
Net pay to employee	X

PAYE

- deduction of income tax due on gross pay
- employer deducts correct amount of income tax for period from gross pay
- employer pays this income tax to HM Revenue and Customs (HMRC).

National Insurance Contributions (NIC)

- two types   – employee's NIC
-                     – employer's NIC
- employee's NIC – deducted from gross pay by employer

                         – paid over to HMRC by employer

- employer's NIC – additional payment to HMRC by employer.

Other possible deductions

- pension contributions
- payments under save as you earn scheme (SAYE)
- payments under give as you earn scheme (GAYE)
- others such as subscriptions to sports/social clubs, trade unions.

Total wages cost

Cost to employer = Gross pay + employer's NIC + employer's pension contributions

Paying wages and salaries

Cash
- very rare
- time-consuming
- security risk

Cheque
- time-consuming
- only practical for small number of employees

Methods of paying wages and salaries

Bank giro credit
- transfer directly to employee's bank account

BACS
- most common method
- transactions recorded on magnetic tape/disc
- processed at BACS computer centre

Example

Gross pay of employee = £500 per week
PAYE = £100 for week
Employee's NIC = £80 for week
Employer's NIC = £90 for week

	£	
Gross pay	500	
Less: PAYE	(100)	Paid by employer to HMRC
Less: Employee's NIC	(80)	Paid by employer to HMRC
Employee's net pay	320	Paid to employee

Employer pays:

	£
Net pay to employee	320
PAYE to HMRC	100
Employee's NIC to HMRC	80
Employer's NIC to HMRC	90
Total cost to employer	590

Total wages cost to employer:

	£
Gross pay	500
Employer's NIC	90
	590

Accounting for wages and salaries

Double entry – two fundamentals

Cost to employer = gross pay + employer's NIC + employer's pension contributions

PAYE and NIC deductions paid over to HMRC by employer

The wages and salaries control account is used to ensure that all wages and salaries costs are correctly paid out to the appropriate parties

Example

Double entry

Gross pay of employee = £500 per week
PAYE = £100 for week
Employee's NIC = £80 for week
Employer's NIC = £90 for week

Step 1 – Gross pay

Debit Wages expense account £590
Credit Wages and salaries control £590
       account

Wages expense account

	£		£
Wages and salaries control	590		

Wages and salaries control account

	£		£
		Wages expense	590

Step 2 – net pay

Debit Wages and salaries control account (£500 – £100 – £80)   £320
Credit Bank account   £320

Wages expense account

	£		£
Wages and salaries control	590		

Wages and salaries control account

	£		£
Bank	320	Wages expense	590

Step 3 – deductions payable to HMRC

Debit Wages and salaries control account (£100 + £80 + £90)   £270
Credit PAYE/NIC account   £270

Wages expense account

	£		£
Wages and salaries control	590		

Wages and salaries control account

	£		£
Bank	320	Wages expense	590
PAYE/NIC	270		

PAYE/NIC account

	£		£
		Wages and salaries control	270

Overall result – balance accounts

Wages expense account

	£		£
Wages and salaries control	590		
		balance c/d	590
	590		590
balance b/d	590		

= total wages cost for period (debit balance = expense)

Wages and salaries control account

	£		£
Bank	320	Wages expense	590
PAYE/NIC	270		
	590		590

= no balance – simply a control account.

PAYE/NIC

	£		£
Balance c/d	270	Wages and salaries control	270
	270		270
		Balance b/d	270

= amount due to HMRC
(credit balance = liability).

CBA focus

The double entries are quite complicated but the key is to use the wages and salaries control account as it should be used, as a check that all costs have been appropriately accounted for.

Paying PAYE and NIC

- payment of amounts deducted and due for PAYE, employee's and employer's NIC made each month
- made by bank giro credit to HM Revenue and Customs
- one payment covering all employees.

Double entry

| Debit | PAYE/NIC account |
| Credit | Bank account |

PAYE/NIC account

	£		£
		Wages and salaries control	270
Balance c/d	270		
	270		270
Bank	270	Balance b/d	270

5

The banking system and bank reconciliations

- Calculating the balance on the cash book.
- Bank statement.
- Cheques.
- Other methods of receiving payment.
- Comparing the cash book and the bank statement.
- Bank reconciliation statement.
- Clearing system.

The banking system and bank reconciliations

Calculating the balance on the cash book

The balance on the cash book at the end of the period is:

Balance on cash book = Opening cash book balance + Cash book receipts total − Cash book payments total

Example

A business had a balance on its cash book at 1 May of £750 debit. During May the cash receipts book shows a total of £5,340 and the cash payments book shows a total of £5,720.

    Balance on cash book at end of May
=   £750 + £5,340 − £5,720
=   £370

KAPLAN PUBLIS

CBA focus

Care must be taken if the opening balance on the cash book is a credit balance (overdraft balance).

Example

A business had a balance on its cash book at 1 May of £750 but this time it was a credit balance or overdraft balance. During May the cash receipts book shows a total of £5,340 and the cash payments book shows a total of £5,720.

> Balance on cash book at end of May
> = -£750 + £5,340 - £5,720
> = £1,130 overdraft

Bank statement

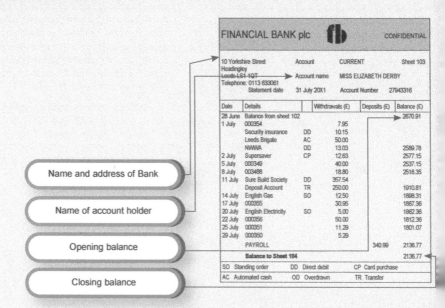

	FINANCIAL BANK plc			CONFIDENTIAL	

10 Yorkshire Street   Account   CURRENT   Sheet 103
Headingley
Leeds LS1 1QT   Account name   MISS ELIZABETH DERBY
Telephone: 0113 633061
     Statement date   31 July 20X1   Account Number   27943316

Date	Details		Withdrawals (£)	Deposits (£)	Balance (£)
28 June	Balance from sheet 102				2670.91
1 July	000354		7.95		
	Security insurance	DD	10.15		
	Leeds Brigate	AC	50.00		
	NWWA	DD	13.03		2589.78
2 July	Supersaver	CP	12.63		2577.15
5 July	000349		40.00		2537.15
8 July	003468		18.80		2518.35
11 July	Sure Build Society	DD	357.54		
	Deposit Account	TR	250.00		1910.81
14 July	English Gas	SO	12.50		1898.31
17 July	000355		30.95		1867.36
20 July	English Electricity	SO	5.00		1862.36
22 July	000356		50.00		1812.36
25 July	000351		11.29		1801.07
29 July	000350		5.29		
	PAYROLL			340.99	2136.77
	Balance to Sheet 104				2136.77

SO	Standing order	DD	Direct debit	CP	Card purchase
AC	Automated cash	OD	Overdrawn	TR	Transfer

Name and address of Bank

Name of account holder

Opening balance

Closing balance

Received periodically from the bank detailing payments and receipts from the account.

Terminology

When you have money in your bank account the bank says you are IN CREDIT.

When you have an overdraft the bank says you have a DEBIT BALANCE.

CBA focus

This terminology may seem to be opposite to that used in the ledger accounts but it is just that the bank statement is looking at the account balance in the bank's point of view. Therefore a debit balance in the business's ledger account means there is cash in the account and this will be called a credit balance by the bank (because the bank owes this to the business) and vice versa.

Cheques

Drawee
the bank upon which the cheque is drawn

Payee
person to whom cheque is written

NATIONAL BANK PLC
18 Coventry Road
Birmingham
B13 2TU

19–14–60
2 / 3 / 20   X1

Pay   J T Tunstill   or order

One hundred pounds only   £ 100.00

Account payee

P DUNSTER

P Dunster

200550   19–14–60   50731247

Cheque number
sequential number pre-printed on cheque

Sort code
identifies branch of bank which issued the cheque book

Account number
drawer's cheque account number

Drawer
person writing the cheque

Checks to make when receiving cheques

Date
cannot be postdated i.e. dated later than today's date
- must be less than 6 months old
  – after 6 months cheques are considered to be out of date

NATIONAL BANK PLC
18 Coventry Road
Birmingham
B13 2TU

19–14–60

2 / 3 / 20   X1

Account payee

Pay J T Tunstill

One hundred pounds only

or order

£ 100.00

P DUNSTER

P Dunster

200550   19–14–60   50731247

Payee's name
must be same as
business account name

Words and figures
must agree

Signature
must be signed
by drawer

Cheque crossings

What is a crossing? Two vertical lines across cheque – usually with words

The 'account payee' crossing is the normal crossing on a pre-printed cheque – it means the cheque can only be paid into the bank account of the payee.

NATIONAL BANK PLC
18 Coventry Road
Birmingham
B13 2TU

19–14–60

20 _____

Pay _____ or order

Account payee

£

P DUNSTER

200550   19–14–60   50731247

Other methods of receiving payment

Automated payments

Standing order regular payments made directly into another bank account

Direct debit allows the supplier to collect varying amounts from customer's bank account on a regular basis

Automated payments

Bank giro credit regular payments made directly into another bank account

BACS large amounts of transactions directly into bank accounts through the BACS computer centre – often used for wages and salaries payments

Credit card and debit cards

Credit card

- purchases made using credit card voucher/PIN
- credit card company pays supplier
- customer pays amounts due to credit card company on regular basis
- amount of purchase must not exceed retailer's floor limit without authorisation from credit card company
- credit card must be in date (start and expiry date).

Debit card

- purchase made using voucher/PIN
- money transferred directly from customer's bank account to supplier's bank account.

Comparing the cash book and the bank statement

When the bank statement is received it should be checked to the cash book to ensure the accuracy of the cash book.

Debits and credits on bank statement

- a debit on the bank statement is a payment
- a credit on the bank statement is a deposit
- this is the opposite way round to the business ledger account as the bank statement is prepared from the bank's point of view.

Procedure

Step 1

- tick off items found in both cash book and on bank statement.

Step 2

- consider the unticked items in cash book and bank statement.

Unticked items in cash book

Items in cash book but not on bank statement

Outstanding lodgements
Cheques paid into bank but not on bank statement yet

Unpresented cheques
Cheques written by business but not cleared onto bank statement

Errors in cash book which cannot be matched to bank statement

The outstanding lodgements and
unpresented cheques are both timing
differences due to the operation of the bank
clearing system. These will be the items
you will need for the bank reconciliation
statement i.e. to prove that the bank
statement and cash book balance agree with
the exception of timing differences.

Unticked items on bank statement

Direct debits/ standing orders
payments made directly out of the bank which have not been entered into cash payments book

Direct credits/ BACS receipts
credits directly into the bank account which have not yet been entered into cash receipts book

Items on bank statement but not in cash book

Bank charges/ interest
not yet in cash book as cashier does not know about them until bank statement received

Errors in cash book
errors such as transposition errors which only come to light when cash book is compared to bank statement

Bank reconciliation statement

Step 1   Compare cash book to bank statement

- covered above.

Step 2   Enter items which are on bank statement but not yet in cash book into the cash book

- typical items include bank charges, direct debits, direct credits or standing orders

- correct any errors in the cash book.

Step 3   Balance amended cash book

- this should give the correct balance on the cash book

- this will not usually agree with the bank statement balance due to timing differences.

Step 4   Prepare bank reconciliation statement

Bank reconciliation statement

	£
Balance per bank statement	X
Less: unpresented cheques	(X)
Add: outstanding lodgements	X
Balance per cash book	X

Once the unpresented cheques and outstanding lodgements have been taken into account the bank statement balance should agree to the amended cash book balance. The cash book and bank statement are reconciled.

Take care again with overdrawn balances. These should be entered as negatives.

Example

A company's cashier has compared the cash book for the month of May to the bank statement at 31 May. The following differences have been noted:

- bank charges on the bank statement not in cash book of £35
- direct debit of £100 on bank statement not in cash book
- cheques written by the business totalling £340 not yet on bank statement
- cheques paid into bank account totalling £200 not yet on bank statement.

The balance on the cash book before this reconciliation took place was a debit balance of £700 but the balance on the bank statement was £705 in credit.

Amend cash book

Cash book

	£		£
Original balance	700	Bank charges	35
		Direct debit	100
		Amended closing balance	565
	700		700
Amended cash book balance	565		

Prepare bank reconciliation statement

	£
Balance per bank statement	705
Less: unpresented cheques	(340)
Add: outstanding lodgements	200
Balance per cash book	565

CBA focus

The bank reconciliation should always be completed using a proforma like the one detailed below.

Although it is usual to see the proforma starting with the balance per bank statement, practise starting with the balance per updated cash book.

Balance per bank statement

    Less:

    Add:

Balance per updated cash book

Clearing system

The major banks have developed a system known as the clearing system which is the method by which the banks process banked cheques.

The whole process of clearing cheques typically takes one working day.

The Cheque and Credit Clearing Company, which manages cheque-clearing in the UK, introduced the Image Clearing System in 2018. Banks and building societies can now process cheques as digital images, so cheques clear faster.

CBA focus

When preparing bank reconciliation statements you will find outstanding lodgements and unpresented cheques which are largely due to timing differences.

Index